THE MASTER GARDENER

A Modern-day Parable
on Inner Healing

by
Laura K. Dahne

The Master Gardener
A Modern-day Parable on Inner Healing
by Laura K. Dahne

Printed in the United States of America

ISBN 978-1-60477-508-2

www.xulonpress.com

TABLE OF CONTENTS

FOREWORD

Dear Reader,

Welcome to the world of the Master Gardener! Enter these pages and as a result you will enter into a modern-day parable on *Inner Healing*. This book is for anyone who has suffered or who has been afraid or ashamed, and truthfully, who among us hasn't? Come join me as together we take a walk through a garden that is as close as your very own heart.

Included at the end of this book is a section titled, *Questions of Reflection*. These questions would be helpful for either personal study or within a group. Following each section of questions is a heartfelt prayer, followed by a special place where you can write your own thoughts and answers.

Special thanks goes out to my wonderful husband Jim, who has always believed in me and my ability to share a story…to all of my amazing children who are my biggest fans…to my faithful niece Rita, who would continually ask, "Are you working on that book, Aunty Laura?!"…to my joy-filled spiritual mom Cary, who is my mentor and role model…and to all of my many supportive friends and family who have cheered me on! But most of all I say, 'Thank you' to Jesus who has loved me in spite of my brokenness and who has turned my heart-holes into *wholeness*!

To you and to them I say, *Happy Gardening!* Laura

> **'Plant the good seeds of righteousness, and you will harvest a crop of love. Plow up the hard ground of your hearts, for now is the time to seek the Lord, that He may come and shower righteousness upon you.' Hosea 10:11-13 NLT**

<u>The Master Gardener</u>

I have a choice to make today:
Who will tend my heart's soil?
Who will offer me comfort?
Who will reward my toil?

Both the Master Gardener and Accuser
Stand ready to till the ground…

I can call the *Master Gardener*
For it's known that He is kind
But change is His requirement
Both a change in heart and mind.

The work of the *Master Gardener*
Is grand beyond compare
But He demands I dig deep
To the very foundations of my garden.

Accuser, on the other hand
Will allow weeds
To grow up with roses
And though his way seems so much easier
I can't help but wonder
What will my garden look like then?

I have a choice to make today:
Who will tend my heart's soil?
Who will offer me comfort?
Who will reward my toil?

Chapter One

A Visitor Comes Calling

I wept! Truly, no other words can be said except these: I wept! *And how could I not?* My garden was a horrible, terrible, awful mess! Oh, to be sure, at one point in time the neighbors might have disagreed, for from a distance my garden *seemed* well-off and healthy, but I knew better. I knew the truth!

It seemed to me that my whole life had been spent in a relentless quest to possess the appearance of the perfect garden. I admit it - I wanted my garden to be admired, desired, and even *envied*! But alas, my desires for these things were continually frustrated. Eventually, in weariness of both body and soul, I scarcely paid attention to whether my packets of seed were in season or out, or if they had in fact already expired; all that mattered was that I show forth a garden that everyone would think was *perfect*.

When my garden wouldn't or couldn't perform to my expectations, which was more often than not, I would find myself furiously ripping up what I had just days before sown, tearing loose from the soil that which I had just previously planted!

Naturally, *inevitably,* after experiencing tremendous guilt about such hateful and ridiculous actions, I would go back once again into my garden and sow seeds, which I would then water with the tears of my bitterness. My heart cried out in despair: *Why can't I achieve a perfect garden?! Everyone else's garden looks so perfect!*

Sometimes late at night, I would lie awake and wonder if there were other gardeners out there who were as anxious about their gardens as I was, or if like myself, they anguished over what they saw in the first rays of morning's light. I often wondered if I was the only one whose garden was not productive, not thriving. Needless to say, as I'm sure *you* can understand, I was much too ashamed to talk to my neighbors about any of this.

As I already stated, there were times I considered speaking to a fellow gardener about my woes - yet that thoughtful consideration would be quickly silenced by a louder, more insistent thought that screamed at me, saying, '*Don't be a fool! So what if your fruit is not maturing…if your garden isn't flourishing? From a distance everything looks perfectly fine. Just keep everyone back, don't let anyone get close enough to tell the difference! Build a fence that's high enough to keep everyone's nosy noses and prying eyes out!*'

And so I am sad to admit that I listened to that demanding inner voice. I built a *continuous-nonstop-unbroken-permanent-fence* around my garden so that others indeed could not see in. On and on it went, day after day, month after month, season after season. Finally, with the *continuous-nonstop-unbroken-permanent-fence* firmly in its place, I returned to the task of achieving the perfect garden.

But for what?! Hardly a flower bloomed and the few trees which did give forth its fruit did so only reluctantly! Simply put: My garden would not flourish! And perhaps even worse was that it seemed as if it *refused* to! My garden's rejection of me as its gardener caused me to churn with humiliation, and with that rejection, my insecurity grew.

So, in desperation I worked even harder, toiling away in the heat of day and oftentimes into the cold of night. And with each new disappointment, and there were so many, I continued to build my fences higher and higher, hoping to hide my ever-deepening shame.

It was at this point, truly the blackest day of my life, when I finally gave in to the awful truth: *My garden was desolate beyond repair! It was nothing less than a waste of my time! I should have never laid seed to such unwilling soil! All that I had done had been for nothing! I would never have a perfect garden!* And so I wept. What else could I do? The whole situation was beyond me, beyond any remedy that I knew of! And if that in-and-of-itself were not bad enough, to make matters *even* worse, I had totally alienated my neighbors. Now I was *totally* alone as well as a *total* failure. And so I wept. *Wouldn't you have, too?*

It is true that there are many types of tears…some sad, some pitiful, some quick and even more quickly forgotten, and some full of great joy. But these new tears I shed were none of those. These tears I cried were hot and angry – these were tears that defied a healing. These were tears of *hopelessness* that had been shut up and locked away for far too long, only now having found a way of escape. These were tears accompanied with deep groaning, for so great was the heaviness of my soul!

It was during this *pity-party-breakdown* that a miraculous thing happened - I made the acquaintance of a stranger, or perhaps it is better said that he made mine. Either way, the truth is simply this: One moment (the most *"horrible-est"* moment of my life!) he was *not* there and the next he just *was*.

The stranger came upon me as I laid face down in the dirt of my unproductive garden…wailing in misery and howling in pain. *Why* he should have bothered to stop and visit a crazed one such as myself continues to bewilder me, but so intense was my heartache on that particular day, that the question of *why* initially never even registered.

If the truth be known, and I intend to be completely truthful, I think it could be more accurately said that I *felt* the presence of the stranger before he spoke a single word. In the very instant that I became aware that I was in fact not alone, he spoke, asking me one simple thing. "Gardener, why do you weep?"

Up shot my head! "Why do I weep?!" I wailed. "Just look around you, stranger! Are you *blind*?!" And with what I am sure was yet another ridiculous display of self-pity, I flailed my arms about as if I were completely mad. I don't know what surprised me more - the fact that I was now temporarily insane or the fact that he didn't seem at all surprised, or even angry for that matter, at my awful outburst!

He simply looked over the expanse of my garden, and gently shaking his head said, "Mmmm....I see you've been busy talking to Accuser. That's too bad. Accuser gives absolutely terrible advice."

Was this stranger barmy? Was my insanity contagious? Who in the roaring blazes was Accuser?

In a huff I replied, "You sir, do not know what you're talking about, for I certainly have *not* been talking to anyone named Accuser! Can't you see that I...*we*, are totally alone here?!"

"Oh, really?" he challenged me kindly. "Then who was it that suggested that you should build your fences so high - or that you should build a fence at all, for that matter? The truth is obvious: While you've been working so hard to keep others out, what you've really done was keep yourself *in*! You've been busy making yourself a prisoner. It's true that others can't get in, but now it seems that you cannot get *out*."

That particular fact embarrassed me greatly; what he said was true! In my haste to hide my awful secret from the world, I had indeed made myself a captive.

Immediately I knew what I must do: Confront him and insist that he leave!

"Well, stranger," I growled, "Since we're on the subject of *getting in*, just how did *you* get in here? I *purposely* provided no door on any of my fences so that I wouldn't be bothered by the likes of you - *uninvited* guests!"

But amazingly, he simply replied, "I don't need a door. I *am* the door."

Now, what in the world did that mean?

Dumbfounded, I tried again. "What I mean to say is that I purposely did not provide a *way* for anyone to get in or out!"

To which he simply replied, "I don't need a way. I *am* the way."

Clearly our conversation was going nowhere!

"Sir," I said quite calmly, although he was truly testing my patience, "As you can clearly see, I am very busy. I have no time for entertaining you or anyone else. If you will now be so kind as to find your way out in the same way that you found your way *in...*"

Chapter Two

Flower Beds

If my uninvited guest heard me at all he obviously chose to ignore me, for rather than leave, he instead walked over to an arid and hideous patch of ground. Once there he began to study it intently. Here he was, up close and personal, looking upon one of my many sources of humiliation: A failed flowerbed! What should have been a glorious display of blue-ribbon chrysanthemums was instead only a bed worthy of being dug up and put to the fire. They were nothing more than dry, spindly, ghastly sticks of wood!

To say that they were in a sorry condition would be an understatement indeed! But oddly enough, the stranger didn't seem to be offended by their ugliness at all. He knelt down beside them, and while I couldn't hear exactly what it was that he was saying, I did catch bits and pieces. He spoke words like *peace… healing…life*. But to who in the world he spoke them to, I had no idea. Certainly even a madman didn't talk to flowers, and dreadful ones at that!

More than a little intrigued, I edged my way over to him, hoping to better hear what he was saying. But no sooner did I reach him that he stood and began to make his way to yet another plot of ground, equally as appalling as the last one. This time though he motioned for me to follow.

Pointing to yet another flower bed failure, he asked, "It was Accuser that suggested you shroud these pansies in bandages, wasn't it?" He was apparently bothered by this for the corners of his mouth turned downward.

I was no less bothered than he, for I had had enough! It was time for me to once again set the record straight. "Sir!" I said in anger, "I don't know who this *Accuser* is that you continually speak of, but I can assure you that covering them up was my idea! They are nothing less than diseased."

"You are right, gardener…" the stranger responded, "But it has been *your* bitterness towards them that have caused them to be so. They have become stressed by your resentment of them; you have cursed them with your hostility. What other response did you expect from them?"

"It's not my fault they're sick and refuse to grow!" I hollered back. "Their ugliness was a constant affront to me, so yes, I covered them! Isn't that what you do with diseased and dying things?"

"No, you shroud *dead* things," he said, "not *dying* things. By wrapping up these little ones you consigned them to darkness. Your little flowers will never find delight in the shadows of gloom, but rather in the light. They have only one desire."

"And what would that be?" I asked him rudely.

With a gentle smile, he answered, "To see the sun."

He then tenderly began to unwrap each of the bandaged-up flowers while he sang a lovely although unfamiliar tune. He worked quietly until every last flower was revealed and showing forth its little drooping head. When finished he let out a slow whistle of approval. He was indeed pleased with himself, yet his pleasure greatly displeased me! How *dare* he undo all my hard work! I should have stopped him the moment he began!

I was very angry with him! Bursting with the need to justify my actions, I cried out while pointing to the newly released, yet still drooping flowers, "Look at them, stranger! I was right to cover them up. They don't appreciate what you've done, not even one little bit! In fact, it's obvious that they are nothing less than *apathetic* to your tender care!" My words were as bitter as my heart.

Surprisingly though, he once again seemed totally undisturbed by my harsh words. *His response?* He simply stood up and went to yet *another* plot of ground - my once beloved rose garden - and began to investigate it. *What in heaven's name, I wondered, was he up to now?*

Chapter Three

Weeds and Roses

A fter examining my rose garden with a careful eye, my guest made his way to my burgeoning tool shed and began banging and clanging and making a frightful noise of it all. *Out came pots! Out came clippers! Out came a spade!* I was terribly tempted to take a peek inside and see just what it was that he might be searching for, but clearly I needed to avoid getting conked in the head! I decided to watch, but only from a safe distance.

After what seemed to be an eternity, he once again appeared, his strong arms laden with all types of gardening equipment and his face wearing a most contented smile. I had to admit, albeit reluctantly, that he seemed to have been born for this very thing;

gardening. With both his tools and smile firmly in place, he headed back once more towards the roses.

Scurrying behind him, I called out, "Sir, just what exactly is it that you intend to do?"

"Heal." he replied.

Heal? *Heal what?*

"I...I don't understand." I responded. And truly I didn't!

He smiled. "I intend to *heal...make well...restore.* This is what I do best, gardener. You could say that it's my specialty."

I was shocked! Was this stranger going to ignore the fact that I had tirelessly slaved over those very same roses? That they had showed their utter contempt for me and my labor by refusing to show forth their beauty? Was he *purposely* trying to embarrass me - once again - by pointing out my failure? Something had to be done!

"Sir!" I warned him. "Your work on those roses will be for naught! There is nothing left to be done for them that I have not tried!"

"Is that so?" He asked me. "Well, let me ask you this, have you sung to them?"

"Well, no."

"Did you read to them?"

"No!" I cried out.

"Hmmm, well then, did you cry over them?" he asked me.

"Of course not!" I exploded. "One does not *sing* to roses or *read* to roses or *cry* over roses!"

"Well then, gardener," he said with a nod and a smile, "you have in fact not done *everything*." Saying this, he turned back once again to the work he had assigned for himself.

"Sir," I cried out angrily. "You are insulting me!"

"Really?" he asked, pausing from his work. "Please trust me when I say that this is never my intention."

"Oh, really!" I hotly replied. "Just what exactly then *is* your intention?!"

And ever so gently and kindly, with his brown eyes fixed on mine, he replied, "To teach you."

"To *teach* me?! To teach *me?*! What in the world do you have to teach me, stranger?" I huffed.

But once again he just smiled. "You'll see. If you'll just be patient, then I'll be able to teach you and you will learn."

"Learn what? *How to sing?* Whoever heard of singing over roses, or reading to roses, or crying over roses? It's beyond the boundaries of sanity, sir!"

"Is it?" he asked me as he once again turned and put his hands to the task before him.

"Sir, I must say it again! *There is nothing left to be accomplished here!* I have given my absolute best to this unruly rose patch, but it has mattered little! They thank me by sending up such tremendous thorns that I would be *mutilated* to even try to tend them! There's nothing left to be done. I can assure you that I have done all that I can do!"

Turning and looking me right in the eye, he simply replied, "I believe you. You have done all that *you* can do. Now it's time for you to let me do what *I* do best."

"And just what is that, sir?" I asked sarcastically.

Undisturbed once again by my apparently unending rudeness, he simply stated, "Save."

Save?! This discussion was going absolutely nowhere! Just how does one argue with a madman... and surely he was mad...wasn't he?

Cautiously he began to cut back the multitude of thorns that grew up in unruly chaos. I decided to sit and watch while I fumed. After all, what was there for me to do? He seemed so intent on *healing* and all. I had already explained to him that my very best efforts had been spent on this same plot of ground.

Let him find out, just like he did with the failed pansy project, how fruitless his work would be and how right I had been all along!

As angry as I was with him (and rightfully so, correct?) I must confess that I couldn't help but marvel how tirelessly he worked or how he kept at his task with a dedication I'd never before witnessed. First, he would snip away at thorns and then he would bend his back to the chore of removing weeds. There was truly such an abundance of weeds growing up in riotous confusion that it was all but impossible to tell where weeds began and rose stems ended!

Not turning away from his work, he spoke to me from over his shoulder. "You never should have allowed Accuser to talk you into planting weeds among these garden beauties. These weeds are choking the life out of your roses."

Again with the Accuser!

"Sir, *I* decided to plant those weeds so that the roses could have companionship!"

"Companionship?!" The stranger laughed. "What in the world do roses have to do with weeds?" he asked. "They're not companions, they're more like enemies. A weed living amongst roses is like gloomy darkness demanding to live with the radiance of light. It can't be done."

I began to respond with a venomous rebuke, yet this time my tongue was silenced, for from his hands dripped a steady, red, river of blood. Long, jagged gashes had etched themselves into both his hands and forearms - yet unbelievably he continued on as if he hadn't noticed.

"Sir!" I hollered. "You are bleeding, and might I add, quite profusely, too!"

But amazingly, surprisingly, he seemed completely unfazed by my news flash. In fact, he behaved as if it were *normal*!

"Yes, I know." he nonchalantly replied. "While it may be disturbing for you to look upon, it's nonetheless of utmost importance. My blood is part of the healing process. Without it, these roses will never reach their full beauty or glory."

"Sir..." I began, taken aback by such a bold and incredible declaration. "I mean no disrespect, truly I don't. But just how in the world does your *bleeding* make a difference?"

"Because life is in my blood." he said.

Life? Life in his blood? Surely he wasn't serious?

He continued, "Yet not just life, but also love."

"*Love*?!" I mocked. "It's maddening that you would declare that these roses need blood, but are you now insinuating that these roses need *love* as well?"

He chose to answer my question with yet another. "Well, let me ask you, gardener, do *you* need love?"

I mumbled that indeed, although it had been a very long time since I'd truly felt loved, that yes, I too needed love.

"Of course you do, gardener!" he said. "And what of nurturing and tenderness, do you have a need for them as well? The answer to all these, most certainly, would be *yes*. It's this way with all created things. *All* things need to be loved…nurtured…tenderly cared for…even roses."

My head was swimming! I had certainly never read anything like this in any gardening handbook!

"But why, sir, would you even bother trying to rescue these roses?" I asked him. "Look at how they have repaid your kindness! They have lashed out at you to prevent you from freeing them!"

Looking down at his bleeding arms, he smiled. "Is that how it appears to you, gardener? Mmmm…I can see why you might think that, yet the truth is they are not *fighting* me, but rather they are clinging *to* me, for they understand that in my hands they will find their deliverance."

He removed a piece of cloth from out of his pocket, and while patting the blood that continued to snake its way down his arm, he instructed me. "Look at this bed of roses, gardener. For just a moment, let the roses symbolize your heart, or more precisely, the *peacefulness* of it. On the other hand, let these weeds represent *bitterness*. Bitterness that perhaps you have felt over past hurts, mistakes and failures – whether they were your own or those of others. Now, just as weeds choke the life out of roses, so bitterness chokes out the peacefulness of a heart."

I was confused! *Singing to roses? Bleeding for roses? Roses of Peace? Weeds of Bitterness?* All of this was too much for a simple gardener such as myself, and for the first time since his arrival I found myself totally speechless.

Dazed, bewildered, and tired, I meandered off to clear my head while he went back to the task of setting roses free. Finding a place to sit where I could watch him from a distance, I confess that as he labored, I dozed - dreaming of clinging roses and gardeners that bled.

I was soon awakened however by a relentless rumble growling in my tummy. I awoke with a start, realizing that the morning had somehow slipped away. I had not eaten, and worse yet, I had not provided any nourishment for my visitor. He may have been *un*invited, but he was nonetheless a guest! Besides, I needed to prove myself to be a better host than I was a gardener!

Still sitting some distance away, I called out to him. "Sir, may I get you a bite to eat?"

"No thanks!" he called out happily. "I have all that I need."

"Are you saying that you're not hungry? It's really no bother to prepare something for you. Perhaps you'd like me to bake us some fresh bread…"

"No, I'm fine." he said. "I have all the bread I need…I'm the bread of all life."

Was he telling me that he had a secret stash somewhere? I thought he was a gardener. Was he now telling me that he was a baker, too?

"Well then, sir, may I get you some cold water?" I hollered out once again.

"No thanks!" he responded. "I have living water right here within me!"

Perhaps it was the heat of the sun or maybe it was because I had gone for too long without food, but truly I could not make good sense out of what my guest was saying! Either way, I gave up. He had clearly said *no*. I would prepare lunch for myself only.

Later, after rejoining him and the work of the roses being finally completed, he stood back to admire what his *love* and *his blood* had accomplished. Where there had once been a jungle of thorns and obscured flowers, there was now only a stunning display of yellow and crimson and pink roses! *But how?* How had he accomplished so much in so little time? *How had he accomplished it at all?*

He must have seen the confusion written plainly on my face, for he gladly answered my unspoken question. "It was only when the weeds were banished that it was possible for the real beauty of your roses to be seen. Their true selves were expressed only when they were finally free from the stranglehold of the weeds."

He had the most mysterious ability to use the gateway of my eyes as a means with which to speak to the very depth of my soul. Looking deep within, he drove the point home. "What's true for these roses is true for you too, gardener. You must never allow weeds of bitterness to choke out the peacefulness of your heart. Don't be deceived into thinking that weeds and roses can live alongside each other. They can't. No more than bitterness and peace can...for bitterness is the enemy of peace."

Chapter Four

Rocks & Stones

*B*itterness and peace were enemies? What a strange idea! But before I had a chance to refute what he'd said, my guest had once again taken off to another part of the garden! This time he headed southward, stopping only long enough to retrieve a pick-axe and a shovel from the tool shed. Being curious, what else could I do but follow, even if I was unsure of him and even more uncertain as to what he was now up to!

Finding a rocky stretch of ground, he paced around it, and after eyeing it carefully, began to take long strides as if measuring the span of it. Then, with a pleased grin brightening his face, he laid aside the shovel and set to work with the pick axe.

Up went the pick axe...d*own* came the pick axe...into hard and unyielding soil! Again and again the axe went *up* with power! Time and time again it came *down* with determination! Except for an occasional grunt, my visitor worked quietly. In just a short while his forehead was drenched in sweat, yet on he worked into the heat of the day...*digging up earth and pulling out rocks... digging up earth and pulling out stones.*

I chose to keep quiet...*but honestly, who was he kidding?!* Wasn't it obvious that although he was certainly working very hard, it was all going to be just a waste of time? Of course, I knew that failure could be the only outcome, for I had already attempted numerous times to prepare that very same ground and make it ready for planting. But as usual, only failure had been my reward. *No siree, not a single seed would ever take hold in that worthless soil!*

Nevertheless, I mused, this time I would just sit back and keep quiet. I would let him see first-hand how mistaken he was and how his labor, sadly, was to be only in vain. Sure, he'd had a stroke of luck with those roses, but this patch of ground? No, he'd never be able to pull it off! Oh to be sure, I was feeling a bit smug, perhaps you could even say that I was a tad 'full of myself' - yet isn't that how people who are in the *right* feel...smug and full?

With that said, you can then perhaps understand my astonishment when unbelievably, undeniably, *incredibly,* that hard and rocky ground did give way to soft, pliable, black dirt! Although my guest didn't seem at all surprised by that occurrence, I certainly was! And to make matters even worse, his expression of pleasure only added insult to my injury...salt to my wound! It wasn't fair! How dare he act as if he knew more about this garden than I did! Once again he had made a fool of me!

As if reading my dark thoughts, my visitor spoke. "This *is* good ground, you know. In fact, it's very valuable ground. But not as it was in its previous condition. First, it had to be broken up...broken up so that it could be made usable."

He paused, as if giving me an opportunity to speak, but I was not going to give him the satisfaction! Besides, the best that I could have mustered up at that point would have been nothing *more* than a growl and nothing *less* than a snarl!

He continued, "Truthfully gardener, the work of properly preparing the ground *had* to be done. In fact, if you would have listened carefully, you would have heard the soil itself crying out, begging to be released from its prison of rocks and stones."

Crying dirt? Prisons constructed of rocks and stones? Oh, brother!

Wiping the sweat from his brow, he again spoke, "These rocks and stones? Think of them as *Stubbornness* and *Pride*. When either one get embedded into the soil, whether the soil of the earth or the soil of the heart, they are merciless. In fact, wherever they make their home, nothing good can grow."

Surveying his work, he smiled and continued, "But once removed? Well, then it's only a matter of time before the ground they came from can once again be healthy."

Looking in my direction, he said, "This is true for you too, gardener. Unless the stony ground of your heart is sufficiently broken up, no good seed will be able to take hold there either."

Pointing to his prized black dirt, he continued. "But, if you're willing, then your heart can become like this new ground, ready for good seed."

I had never heard such an outrageous thing! Was he implying that I had a stony heart? Worse yet, was he suggesting that my heart was embedded with Stubbornness...with Pride?!

Gazing upon his work once again with a nod of pleasure, he invited me to recline with him on a nearby patch of grass, one that was thankfully bathed in shadow. It was a good thing too, because I was already hot...at least under the collar, so to speak! *And why not? Hadn't he completely disregarded everything I'd told him about this garden? Hadn't he totally overlooked the fact that I had spent count-less seasons toiling away in it? And just who was he anyway, barging into my garden the way he did? And, no sooner having arrived, hadn't he begun to tear apart my carefully constructed world! Sure, it was a poorly-constructed world and it was a lonely world, but nonetheless it was MY world! How could I not be angry? After all, I was the gardener of this garden! I...*

And then...like a thunderbolt...it hit me: *I, I, I, Me, Me, Me, Mine, Mine, Mine!* These were my favorite words, or so it appeared, since I seemed to love using them so much! *Oh, my goodness!* Could I indeed be filled with...*gasp*...Pride?! Was *Pride* the reason I had rejected everything he had said...why I resisted his extraordinary, albeit bizarre, gardening abilities? No! There *had* to be another reason...a logical reason, a legitimate reason. There was only one little problem: I couldn't think of a single one!

Chapter Five

Conflict

And so the conflict began. Moment by moment it grew. And just as a hungry flame rapidly grows into a ravenous fire when met with the proper kindling, so it was with the bitter thoughts warring within me. I needed to get away and clear my head! I needed to go somewhere and think!

And so it was that I fled the stranger's presence in hopes of stopping the noise that was raging within my skull. I found myself running from place to place inside my garden, looking for a spot where I could find a reprieve, but there was no place in which I could find the rest I longed for. The problem? Wherever I went, there *I* was! And it was becoming apparent that perhaps, *egads*, I was my biggest problem!

And so the conflict raged on and on and on.

It raged within my head...
It raged within my heart...
It raged and raged and raged!

I turned my clamoring thoughts over and over as one might find themselves turning over autumn leaves, examining them from both sides. *But what exactly was it that I was looking for?* Answers or Excuses? Justifications or Explanations?

As I walked, I fumed and as I fumed, I walked. I was right, wasn't I? I mean, I'd put up with his trying to show off with the chrysanthemums (even though they were surely a lost cause!) and I'd even dealt with him making a mess of my tool shed, but now *this*? To imply that I was somehow Stubborn, somehow Prideful? I mean really, hadn't he gone too far?

And it was at that moment of serious self-justification that I saw *them*.

The pansies...
But not as they had been.
Now they were radiant.

And as if caught in the throes of worship, their little heads were pressing *up, up, up*, as if longing to embrace the sun and shower it with little, velvety kisses.

My heart lifted and sank all at the same time – for once again he had been right…and I'd been wrong! Those pansies had not been hopeless after all, only I'd been hopeless! Everything I had desired for my garden hadn't been borne of a desire for anyone or anything other than myself – it had all been for me, myself and I! I hadn't wanted perfect pansies for the sake of the pansies; I'd only wanted their perfection so that I might gloat. I now saw so very clearly how my actions had been harsh and unkind towards my garden…and how it had faded under my constant, unforgiving criticism.

And so it was that for the second time that day, I wept. Oh, to be sure, these were very different tears, but nevertheless they were tears that were as difficult as the first. Even though I truly, honestly, sincerely, wanted there to be another reason of *why* I felt so angry towards my visitor - of why I was so offended by him, the answer was sadly becoming more and more painfully clear: My hardened, offended heart was crammed full of Pride! It was *angry* that he was able to do what I couldn't! It was *insulted* that what was hard for me to accomplish was easy for him! And with those admissions finally made, I was at last able to see my compulsive need to always point the finger-of-blame in the direction of others, for what were in truth, my own failures, my own shortcomings.

As I knelt beside the bed of pansies, beholding their glorious transformation made possible only by the stranger, I had no choice but to surrender to the awful truth: I was torn…torn between my desire to hate him and my desire to learn more of him!

And though I was loath to admit it, my jealousy of him *(oh no…jealousy, too?!)* was not enough to extinguish my curiosity about him! And so I can safely say that it was then, at that very moment, that I decided to accept the fact that although I *hadn't* invited him, he was nonetheless in my garden!

The most paralyzing thought of all? *If I were to reject him, to whom else could I possibly turn?!* Hadn't I come to the absolute end of my own hope? I needed him! Surely he would provide a new supply of what I so desperately had need of - hope! Oh, as much as Pride would reject him, I was in no position to. He, and he alone, had what I needed - *answers*! It was then that I again resolved within my gardener's heart that from that point on I would welcome his help…no matter how strange or peculiar it might be! Perhaps what he had implied about me was right after all: Maybe the barrenness of my garden was in fact nothing less than a reflection of me.

Maybe, just maybe, I did have something to learn. Perhaps I did need a teacher after all.

And for the first time ever, without warning, I began to experience a new kind of shame - the disgrace one feels when their self-righteous heart has been exposed – laid bare – for its owner to see! And though this shame was, like the other form I was sadly so familiar with, sharp and cutting to the core, it was different...it was cleansing...and it pointed me in the direction of seeking forgiveness. I knew that immediately I must apologize to the stranger! I knew that no longer was it an option to regard him as *uninvited*, but rather as a welcomed guest.

And queerly enough, just like that, with the decision having been firmly made to seek reconciliation with the stranger, the warfare within came to an immediate cease-fire and a truce was thankfully, *mercifully* declared!

Chapter Six

Seeds

L et it be known for the record that upon my return, the stranger, or rather, my *welcomed guest* was to me the very epitome of kindness. It seemed as if there was no end to his abilities, *kind-heartedness* being just one of the many attributes that he displayed to me that day.

I'd found him exactly where I'd left him, and if in fact he was at all bothered by my abrupt departure, he surely didn't show it. With red-rimmed eyes and a stuttering tongue, I poured out a heart-felt apology. In return, I was rewarded with the most tender smile I'd ever had the pleasure to receive. It would perhaps be impossible for me to tell you which held greater warmth - those eyes of his or that engaging smile – but suffice it to say that they were both ablaze with compassion. And while it may very well be an under-statement to say that I was, and *am,* grateful for his excusing my rudeness that day, it is nevertheless a statement that demands to be made.

Poking at the ground with my toe, I tried desper-ately to think of some clever way to persuade him to continue on with his lesson. After all, who could blame him if he decided to call it quits with me? Yet, once more he proved himself kind, and as one might expect, he didn't make me beg.

"So, by removing those rocks and stones," he said, as if there had never been a break in our conver-sation, "I was really removing *barriers....*barriers which kept the soil from becoming all that it was meant to be. The work is tedious, that's true, but a good gardener always, in advance, takes into account the amount of labor that will be necessary to make the ground usable."

"How can a gardener possibly know how long it will take?" I asked, relieved that the teaching had once again began.

"Mostly by experience," he responded. "Yet, as important as it is for the gardener to take into account the *amount* of work that is ahead, the wise gardener must also have within him a *vision.*"

"A vision? Of what?" I asked.

"Of what the end result will be…a vision of the desired outcome! *Accounting* and *Vision,* working together as a team, will give the gardener the encouragement necessary to continue on, despite the many hardships that will occur."

"Hardships?" I gulped.

"Sure, because wherever there is transformation, there are growing pains as well." Kneeling down and taking up a handful of soil, he continued, "In the same manner that the gardener needs encouragement, the ground needs something as well: Assurance that the work of liberation that was begun in it will continue…"

"For how long?" I interrupted.

"Until the gardener has made it ideal for planting." He replied.

"Why?" I asked.

"Because *liberation* is often a painful work. When the ground, whether of the earth or of the human heart, has been given assurance that the gardener will not stop in the midst of the process – but will instead carry on until the work is done - it is then given the ability to *endure*!

"A good and wise gardener must have not only patience, but must also be willing to bring, at whatever the cost, liberty to the places where rocks and stones once ruled."

He remained silent for a bit, perhaps in a desire to give me the time needed to digest such a wealth of new knowledge. Although I appreciated the window of silence, I nonetheless found myself hungering for what his next words might be.

Setting the soil back down in its place, he continued, "Now that this ground has been properly prepared, you'll of course need to plant good seed. But it's vitally important that the seed you sow be the *right* seed so that you can bring in the *right* harvest. Should you decide to sow seeds of corn it will be a harvest of corn you reap. Likewise, should you decide to sow seeds of wheat, it will be a harvest of wheat that you will reap. Sow wisely, gardener, for whatsoever you sow today is what you will eat of tomorrow."

"So my choice of seed is that important?" I asked.

"Extremely..." he replied, "but it's not just your *choice* that's important, but also the *quantity* you choose. Plant abundantly and you will reap abundantly; plant sparingly and you will reap sparingly."

I thought back to the countless times I'd withheld sowing Abundance, simply out of fear that it might never take root. No wonder Scarcity had been my only return!

"Gardener, what I'm saying in regards to the ground of your *garden*, I'm saying is true for the ground of your *heart*, too."

"In what way?" I asked him.

"Well, your thoughts are your seeds. Whatever you continually think on becomes what you believe, and what you come to believe will eventually show itself in the way you behave...in the choices you make.

"It works like this - sow thoughts of Gratitude and you will surely reap a harvest of good works that reveal a grateful heart. But by the same measure, should you unwisely choose to sow thoughts of Stubbornness, you would in time gain a stubborn heart, which would be clearly revealed through your actions. Therefore, you must be very careful what seed you choose to sow, which thoughts you choose to think, and in what quantities you choose for both."

I promised him I would be very careful.

"And one more thing, gardener," he concluded with a smile, "When you sow seed in your garden, sow enough to give away when your harvest comes in. The truest joy of being a gardener is having enough left over to share with others."

Chapter Seven

Boulder-dash

My guest stood up and treated himself to a much deserved stretch. I followed his lead.

"Do you see that boulder over there?" he asked me, squinting at an object across the way. Dutifully, I scanned the surrounding area. After assuring him that I did indeed see it, he asked me, "Does that boulder signify something that is useful or something that is a hindrance to your garden?"

What was he asking me!? I'd never contemplated the mysteries of a boulder before!

"Umm...uh..."

Perhaps this was a trick question! Perhaps my guest was just having some fun with me! That thought however was quickly quelled by the seriousness written on his face. Goodness, I didn't want to disappoint my guest, but truly this question was much too hard! How in the world was I going to find an answer regarding the mystery of the hulking rock that sat heavy in my garden!

"Well, sir..." I began, "I guess it could be a... um...what I mean to say is that perhaps it's a...my best guess is that, uh..."

Oh goodness, I was failing miserably! Perhaps he would rescue me from this impossible situation by just telling me what it meant!

Instead of providing me with an answer however, he just smiled one of his radiant smiles, picked up the nearby shovel, and walking over to where the hulking piece of stone was, began to dig a trench around it. Round and round he went, much like the thoughts in my head. *What was he trying to show me? Perhaps if I studied hard enough I could figure it out!*

After digging down about three feet on every side, he stepped back, and wiping his brow, asked me. "Well, have you decided gardener? Is the boulder useful or something that is a hindrance? Should it stay or go?"

My heart was pounding with uncertainty and sweat was forming on my upper lip. Yet, suddenly, wonderfully, an answer bubbled up from somewhere deep within me! *But could it really be the right answer?* Bracing myself, I blurted out, "It's neither! It's *both*!"

"And should it stay or go?" he asked me with a smile.

"It should...let's see now...it should *stay*!" At this point I was so delighted for having an answer, especially one that wasn't being *laughed* at, that I nearly did a jig right there on the spot. "But, it shouldn't stay where it is!" I cried out. "It should be...it should be moved!"

Now what did I mean by that? Just how does one go about moving a boulder?!

"You've answered correctly!" he replied, obviously happy with me and my answer. "It's true gardener, the boulder is neither good nor bad, but rather it's the *location* of it that determines whether it should stay or go.

"As it is right now, this boulder sits heavy in the ground. Whereas it is its' *heaviness* that dooms it to sit where it is, it is its' *positioning* that forces it to suffer the heat of the sun and become exceedingly hot. No *one* or no *thing* can find rest on it or even beside it because its heat burns like a raging fever.

So, although it has great potential as a place for one to find rest..." He allowed his words to trail off.

"This weighty stone, gardener, is just like Anger that sits heavy in the heart. They both burn with such an intense heat that it completely drives others away. Just as heaviness and heat doom this boulder, so too does the heaviness and the heat of Anger doom the human heart."

He motioned for me to join him and we began the arduous task of removing the heavy rock from its home. And by gosh, bit by bit, we did move it! Inch by inch we were able to budge it enough until finally we were able to remove it completely! My guest wiped his sweltering brow and continued his gardening lesson.

"Anger is an emotion which, like this boulder, can be good or bad."

"How's that?" I asked, very curious.

"Because *Righteous* Anger is just what it implies: Anger that is blameless. This type of Anger should live within everyone's heart."

"But how can anger be *blameless*?" I asked.

"It is found to be without fault when it seeks to honor others and not itself. Righteous, blameless anger flames at the sight of inhumanity, injustice and unkindness shown towards others. Righteous Anger takes no thought for itself, but rather stands up to defend and protect those in harm's way. On the other hand however, Anger, when it is self-centered, cares only for itself. Its' selfishness and feverish rage work together to drive away all that would dare to come near.

"Now that we've freed this boulder, we're going to move it to a place where it won't have to burn hot all day. Once we do, once we position it in a place of shade, it will then become a place of comfort, both for itself and for others."

Giving me a friendly wink, he concluded the lesson. "Likewise gardener, let *your* Anger sit only in the shaded places of your heart, allowing your heart to become a place where others can find refreshment from the furious heat and troubling cares of this world."

I marveled at how his reasoning could be so simple and yet so complex! Who knew that there was so much to know about gardening?!

Chapter Eight

Roots, Tending Them

Just as my guest had said, together we did find the boulder a new and better home. We were awarded with a soft and cooling breeze that refreshed us as we prepared to take a break from our hard labor. Although my guest seemed hardly winded, I was hurting in every conceivable place! Since he had worked practically non-stop since first arriving, I asked him how he was feeling.

"Excuse me sir," I asked, "but aren't you exhausted?"

He smiled, "No, not really. I never tire of tending to my father's business."

Was his father a gardener too, I wondered?

"What do you mean sir, by 'your father's business'?" I asked.

"*You*," he said with a laugh, "are my father's business!" On that puzzling note, he sat down, closed his eyes and leaned back against the newly placed boulder.

Did I even know who his father was?

Time passed by pleasantly as we rested and yet…I found my heart becoming anxious. I couldn't help but wonder if he was nearly done with the work in my garden. Yes, he had accomplished amazing things in the short time he'd been there, and for that I was most grateful. However, as my eyes surveyed the rest of my *un-yet-un-touched* garden, my heart sank for there was still so much more that remained to be done! But certainly asking him to stay longer was out of the question. He had already given me so much of his help, how could I possibly ask for more? *Besides, I shuddered to think what his bill would be for services already rendered!*

After a short while, my guest opened his eyes and surveyed my garden with great intensity. *What was he up to this time, I wondered?* Finally, he broke the silence. "See that apple tree over there, gardener?" he asked me, pointing to a tree that stood just a few yards to my left. I replied that I did.

"I know that up to now you haven't been able to harvest any fruit from it, but it isn't for the reasons you've suspected. You've always believed, incorrectly I might add, that the answer to the health of that tree was found in its leaves and limbs."

"Well, if not there, sir, then just where *does* the answer lie?" I asked.

"In its *roots*!" he declared.

"It's roots?" I croaked.

"Yes! Its *roots* are the key to its health. Usually gardeners attempt to treat symptoms…and truthfully, that's been your mistake as well in dealing with this tree."

"I don't follow…" I confessed.

"It's simple really - you've invested all your energy into the caring of the leaves and the trimming of the limbs. But since these areas don't hold the key to its health, no real solution could be found. What this tree needs, gardener, is *nourishment*!"

Nourishment?

"Nourishment to its very roots, for out of its *roots* the wellspring of its life will come! Hear me well, once the roots are well-fed, then healthy fruit will be its reward."

Well-fed roots?

"I promise you, this tree will produce abundant life when its roots receive the nourishment they need from living water!"

Living water!?

"Sir," I asked, feeling a bit overwhelmed (and quite embarrassed that I once again had no idea what he was talking about!) "How do I go about *nourishing* roots? They're so far down! How can I ever hope to affect what I can't even see?"

"Oh, but you *do* see them!" he answered. "You see them every day by the *evidence* of what they produce. Every day you're a witness to the well-being of the roots just by looking at what is going on in the limbs, the leaves, and the bark."

As puzzling as this was to me, I paid very close attention.

"Sir, you speak of *living water*. Are you saying I just need to water this tree more?"

"Simply, *yes*..." he responded. "And simply, *no*."

"Huh?"

Kindly laughing at my obvious show of confusion, he explained, "Well, while it's true that you do need to water, it's really what you water *with* that matters the most. If you use polluted water, well then you can only expect polluted roots, but..."

"But if I use good, clean water I get good, clean roots, right?" I interrupted, happy to finally be getting it!

My guest beamed with joy. "Exactly, gardener! Now let me ask you, where is the water supply you've been using to water your garden?"

Gulp!

"Well sir," I began "not uh, understanding the need for my garden to have, umm, living water and all, I simply used...ahhh, I mean I...umm..." and rather shame-facedly I was resigned to just pointing in the direction of the back of my humble abode.

"Take me there." he said.

I dreaded every step because I just knew he would disapprove! And now that I knew better, could I blame him?

I walked with him over to where my watering hole was, but truthfully we smelled it even before we reached it! The stench of stagnant water was heavy in the air. *Simply put...Yuck!*

"Gardener, is *this* your water supply?" he asked me incredulously. "Are there no other places from which you can draw water?!"

Mumbling, I replied, "Well sir, I *could* go to a different pond but it's located much farther back in the garden and this pond was so much more convenient that I thought it surely was a good choice, saving me time and all. After all, water is only water, right?"

Even as I said it, I confess that I didn't really believe it! At least not anymore. Since his arrival I'd come to realize that nothing was as it seemed, therefore water indeed must be more than only water.

"The *source* of water you choose is always important." he admonished me. "Although it may have been *easier* for you to draw water from here, it certainly was not *wiser*. In fact, it cost you more in the long run…more work, more frustration, more tears; not to mention what that poor tree has been deprived of!" Though his words pierced me, he laid a gentle hand on my drooping shoulders and encouraged me with his following words, "Come, let's go and find some fresh water so that we can tend to the roots of that apple tree."

With my heart once again lifted, we ambled over to the now-nearly-emptied tool shed and hunted for buckets that were suitable for gathering *living water*. Finding some, we headed to a pond in the back yard (which I suddenly realized was really not *that* far away!) and gathered fresh water from it. After we once again made our way to the base of the apple tree, we gently and slowly poured the life-giving water into the ground and watched the thirsty soil drink it in.

"Sir, how will I know when I have given it enough?" I asked.

"You'll only know by paying careful attention. Begin by feeding it a reasonable amount, and then day-by-day carefully observe it, all the while asking, *'Is my tree flourishing? Is there good fruit as a result? How do the limbs, the leaves, and the bark look?'* These questions will give you the answers you need in knowing whether you have watered too little, too much, or just enough."

He continued on. "The roots of this tree are an illustration of the roots that are anchored in you. If your roots are watered with poison then everyone else will know it by your leaves, your limbs and your bark."

"I...I don't understand," I said for what seemed like the hundredth time. "How can *I* have leaves, limbs and bark?"

"It's simple, really. Just as you can't see the roots of this apple tree, neither can the world around you see your roots. What they *do* see is leaves which are your *words*… limbs which are your *actions*…and bark which signify your *attitudes*. Your words, your actions, and your attitudes will show you, and others, whether your roots are soaking up pure or poisoned water."

"But where are *my* roots, sir?" I asked.

"Your roots are in your mind, where your thoughts live. Are your thoughts good or wicked, gardener? Are your thoughts anchored in truth or in lies? Remember, poisoned water produces poisoned roots and pure water produces pure roots. Therefore, *depraved* thoughts produce depraved words, actions, and attitudes. *Wholesome* thoughts, on the other hand, produce wholesome words, actions, and attitudes."

I wondered what my heart had been watered with most recently and the answer struck me with great force: Fear! *My mind had been drenched in fear!* And that fear had driven me to depression and despair! I then began to reflect on my past thoughts and I saw how they had indeed influenced my behaviors. Oh, I could clearly see that once again my visitor knew just what he was talking about!

"The choice every gardener must make is an extremely important one." he said. "From what source will they water their roots? You see, the health of their harvest will be dependent on that one choice.

"What about you, gardener?" he asked me pointedly. "What water source will you now draw from on a daily basis? Will it be from ponds of pure, living water or from murky, stagnant ponds?"

Sensing that it was only a rhetorical question, I chose to remain silent.

Chapter Nine

Roots, Removing Them

What water source would I drink from now? This question became a song that danced about in my head. I resolved right then and there that from that moment on I would feed my mind good and worthwhile thoughts! After all, I knew what the alternative held and it was *not* appealing!

My guest smiled at me. "You've chosen well! Just as you can't plant seeds of *Fear* and hope to harvest *Courage,* you can't hope to keep good seed alive with tainted waters."

I hadn't realized that I'd spoken out loud! I mean, I had, hadn't I? How else…

"Now, come follow me, gardener…" he said, "And tell me what you think about this patch of ground." I of course followed him to the place where he wanted me to go.

"Well, sir, there really isn't much to tell." I said, standing beside him. "Suffice it to say that some time ago I made the decision to not plant anything in this here soil. I'd been so busy with so many other things that I just sort of hoped that something, *anything*, would take root on its own and perhaps someday surprise me. But as you can see, except for these straggling and struggling weeds..."

My guest shook his head at this admission and then patiently explained the foolishness of my thinking. "Gardener, you must sow seed before you can ever hope to see evidence of a harvest. It would be unwise for a gardener to wait for cucumbers to grow if not even one cucumber seed has been planted! There is a law at work within the world and it is this: You will reap a good harvest *when* you sow. But, oftentimes *no* seed is ever planted yet a plentiful harvest is expected!"

He continued. "I caution you: Any ground left unsown long enough *will* become a home, but only to wild plants and unruly weeds. When that happens, it will only be after many countless hours of labor that you will then be able to remove them. It is better to first plant what you *do* want than to spend your days removing a harvest you *don't* want. You are the gardener, and you have been given the charge and responsibility for your own garden. You must be wise in what you allow to take root in your soil."

My guest was again teaching amazing and marvelous truths that I had never heard before!

Pointing to a nearby lemon tree, he motioned for me to walk with him towards it. "I've taught you the importance of watering properly in order to nourish roots, but now I want to teach you yet another thing."

I was hesitant to go; I truly was, for my lemon tree was a source of disgrace for any gardener, good or not! It had never once produced a single lemon!

Laying his hand upon the tree, he said, "Sometimes, for various reasons, roots cannot thrive where they are. Therefore, with great care, they must be dug up."

"Dug up?" I asked. "*Why?*"

"Because the tree's very purpose is that it would produce. Therefore, it must be given every opportunity to thrive. I am going to take an ax to this tree but it will be for the sole purpose of uprooting it from its current home and moving it to a more promising one.

I want you to understand that for every created thing, *Life* is always to be the first option."

Continuing, he said, "I will then replant this unfruitful tree by a body of pure water so that it will then have every chance to flourish. There its roots will have every opportunity to grow deep and its leaves will have no reason to wither."

"Sir, this is a very lucky tree!" I rejoiced.

"Yes, I agree." he smiled. "But, after all of that, if it still does not bear fruit, in spite of all the special care and consideration that it has been given, then and only then would it be found worthy of being chopped down completely."

"Completely?" I gasped.

"Completely, for then it would be apparent that it failed only because of its *unwillingness* to provide what it was created for."

"Which is?"

"To serve…to serve others, as well as to serve the gardener who planted, lovingly nurtured, and tirelessly cared for it."

He smiled a splendid smile. "Now, once the tree is properly situated, then the thoughtful gardener will begin the process of pruning. The gardener prunes so that the tree will mature properly. But watch out!

When that tree receives its pruning, it really is quite a sight! Its long limbs are cut back to mere stubs, and later, the first promises of its fruit will be quickly gathered up and removed."

"That sounds harsh, sir!"

"Well, while it may *sound* harsh, these actions are nothing less than a show of concern for the tree and its future potential. It is the gardener who *loves* his tree that will cut back the excess so that the tree can be *more*."

"More? *More than what?*" I asked.

"More than it ever dreamed it could ever become." he answered.

"Is it so that the tree can become big and strong?" I asked.

"Sure, but that is certainly not the main reason. Although strength *is* a valued quality, it is not the attribute that's of greatest importance, gardener."

"Then what is?" I asked.

"The willingness to serve. *That* is the quality that's to be highly desired."

"Sir, am I like this lemon tree?" I asked.

With delight he answered, "Absolutely! For just as this fruit tree must be willing to bear fruit, so too must you be willing to bear fruit."

"But how can *I* bear fruit?" I balked. "I'm not a tree!"

"It's simple," he laughed, "Just as the tree is expected to serve others, so are *you*. This is how you bear fruit…you serve. But, in order for you to properly serve, you must first posses the greatest tools known, Truth and Love. What fertilizer is to a lemon tree, that's what Truth and Love are to the gardener."

"Wow, they sound *really* important." I said.

"Oh, they are! In fact, every gardener, if he is wise, will invest *everything* into those two things."

"Invest *everything* into?" I gulped.

"Yep, everything…" he said, "for they are of the greatest value!"

"But, sir, what will it cost *me* to have them?" I asked.

"Everything!" he replied cheerfully.

"Everything?" I again gulped.

"Yes, *everything!*" he replied softly.

My tummy rumbled again, but it wasn't for lack of food this time! No, this time my tummy was growling with anxiety for I was not wealthy! How would I ever be able to afford what I needed the most when I did not have the resources to do so?! Here he was telling me that what was of the greatest value I could never possibly possess! As my heart broke, a tear slipped down my cheek.

Drawing close, he gently said to me, "Friend, while it is true that it will cost you *everything,* it will also cost you *nothing.* The great debt of owning them has already been paid for."

"By who?" I trembled. *I didn't know of anyone who could pay my debt for me!*

"It's been paid for in full by The Master Gardener." he said.

"Who...who's that?" I asked, confused.

"The Master Gardener is the one who walks the gardens of the world, setting things right and restoring what has been lost. Through a transaction called Sacrifice he has purchased Truth and Love for all that would desire to have them. What cost him everything, he gives away freely. There is however one requirement..."

"And what is that?" I asked.

"That you receive the free gifts of Truth and Love with a grateful and joy-filled heart."

Oh, my heart was indeed grateful to hear such extraordinary news! Filled with Joy to know that I could in fact possess what was of the greatest value!

"Come," he said, "it's getting late…let's take care of that lemon tree."

Chapter Ten

And The Walls Came Tumbling Down!

As we made our way back from the challenging work of uprooting and moving the lemon tree to a better home, we found ourselves face-to-face with a portion of my *continuous-nonstop-unbroken-permanent-fence*.

"It's time…" he said simply.

"Time? *Time for what?*" I asked.

"Time," he said, "to take down this monstrous wall."

Immediately I felt my heart sink! Where would we even begin? I had built my fences up so high; it now seemed nothing short of impossible to take them back down!

"Don't be afraid of what you *see,* gardener. Instead, go by what you *know*! For instance, how is it that you were able to build such imposing fences in the first place?" he asked me.

"Well, one board at a time, sir…" I replied.

"Exactly, and that is precisely how we'll take them *down*...one board at a time."

I was greatly encouraged to hear that!

With our plan in place, we headed one last time back to the tool shed. He searched until he found what he was looking for, a sledgehammer, and then walked back to where we'd been. I lingered a little longer, looking for something with which I could use for the work that was ahead. Finally, upon doing so, I hurried over to join him.

Whomp! Whomp! Whomp! Lifting the powerful sledgehammer above his head, my guest began the chore of demolishing the *continuous-nonstop-unbroken-permanent-fence* that had become my prison wall. I looked at what he held…I looked at what I held…and I realized just how pitiful the little hammer was that I was holding in my hand! Certainly my vision for taking down the wall had been much too small, certainly much smaller than his!

Seeing my distress, he quickly and quietly calmed me with his next words. "Do not overlook the seemingly insignificant, gardener, for it is often the small things that are linked to the mighty! Such is the case with your hammer. You see that hammer as insignificant for the task at hand, and yet it's exactly what you need! That hammer you hold can get into places that a sledgehammer never could! Sure, that hammer can't *whomp* heavy fence posts, but it sure can remove driven nails!"

My heart swelled, my courage grew and my little hammer began to feel more significant by the minute!

"Don't be discouraged, gardener, when what you hold in your hand doesn't seem to be enough. Offer it up in faith and it will *become* enough. With confidence, use *whatever* is in your grip...and it will *always* be enough to get the job done!"

We returned once more to the work before us, occasionally laughing and singing a familiar song or two. We labored together gladly for quite some time. He *whomped* while I pulled nails and together we made a great team. Deep down I knew that he could've taken care of the whole affair himself and in probably half the time, too! Nonetheless, I felt honored that he allowed me, in fact *welcomed* me, to help him at all.

Bit by bit, board by board, the more the walls came down, the more I began to see the marvelous glory that I had blocked out of my life! My hungry eyes *feasted* on the unending splendor before me! Stately oaks and elegant elms seemed to be waving glad greetings of hello with their leafy arms. To the west, I could almost *hear* the neighbor's bougainvilleas screaming with pure delight as they contemplated the beauty of their purple magnificence. A bit further down there was crotons and tulips and pansies and posies to behold! So much color, so much pleasure for my eyes to see! And to think that I had hidden myself away from all of this breathless display! I vowed that I would never be guilty of such a terrible thing again.

As I looked at all of the beauty that now surrounded me, my mind raced over the innumerable lessons that my guest had taught me and how I was forever changed by his visit. *How was it, I began to wonder, that he had known to come to me in the darkest hour of my life? How had he heard about my distress in the first place? And how in the world had he gotten in at all, for truly, as I was painfully becoming more and more aware of, I had built nothing less than a great divide between myself and others!* As I pondered these wonderful things, I greatly suspected that even if I were to ask, that I would never fully grasp the answers; I was learning that the simplest things in the gardens of life often held the greatest mysteries.

As my thoughts continued to wander, my guest and I continued to labor. Eventually, many hours later, we began to stack all the wood we'd removed from the torn down walls. It created, as you might imagine, a tremendous, gigantic, incredible pile!

As if rewarding us for our back-breaking labor, the sun painted the sky with the most magnificent display of reds and blues as it began its westward descent. My guest took some quiet and reflective moments to observe the evening's glory so vividly displayed. In doing so, I heard him quietly offer up a word of thanks. I had never before taken time to notice the coming night, much less offer up appreciation for it, but that time I did, and I knew that from that moment on I always would.

Looking once again at the mountain of wood we'd gathered, I gulped! "What shall we do with it all?" I asked.

"We're going to set it on fire!" he said. "We're going to let it burn until there's nothing left to remind you of your former disgrace or pain."

From his pants-with-many-pockets *(was this, I wondered, where he also kept his stashes of bread and living water?)* he pulled out a packet of matches, and with a brilliant smile, laid a flame to the mountain of wood. The fire caught quickly and began to spread rapidly. We both watched in awe at the spectacular sight before us. *Emancipation* was having its very own celebration bonfire!

Oh, what a day, what a day, I mused! I was bushed, yet elated…tired, yet refreshed…pooped out, but not done in! And as we stood together and watched the sparks from the fiery blaze make their way up into the heavens, I felt fulfilled with all that had taken place throughout the day.

My guest reached out, and touching my shoulder announced, "We've accomplished much today, gardener." His words resonated with pleasure, were deep with satisfaction.

"Well, truthfully sir," I blushed, "I know that you could have done all of this on your own. I know you didn't really need *me* to help."

His eyes brightened. "But I did need you, gardener! I'm *always* able to accomplish infinitely more whenever there's teamwork. Although it's a fact that I can do *everything*, without your cooperation, I would have in fact been able to do *nothing*. Your Trust, partnered with my Wisdom, produced all that you see - and even *more* than you can see right at this moment."

I beamed!

Pointing to the homes that dotted the now beautifully-seen-landscape, he sighed. "Gardner, it's been far too long that you've kept yourself hidden away. There are others out there who are weighed down with secret shame regarding the condition of their gardens. It's up to you to go to them…to console them."

But sir, how do I even begin?" I asked.

"You begin," he said, "by telling them the truth – of you and your garden. Your struggles and troubles will give you the credibility needed for them to listen to you. Now go and teach them what I've taught you. Share with them everything that I've feely shared with you."

Gulp!

83

"Sir, I promise to do everything you've said…
but you mention that you *'have freely given to me'*
and um…well, sir, even though I have very little
with which to offer you, certainly you must take
some form of payment for all that you've done for
me!" Looking wildly about my garden, I tried to find
something, *anything*, of value to give to him.

"Gardener," he said gently, "you have already
given me the only payment I really desire."

"I have?" I asked amazed. "*And what is that?*"

"Your heart."

"My heart?"

"Yes…for when one gives their heart, they in
truth give everything."

He was right! I *had* given him my heart…and my
confidence too! *And why not? He'd shown himself
worthy of both!* He had come, seeking only to help,
and wonder of wonders, he had asked for nothing in
return! Yes, I *would* go to my neighbors, especially
the ones with really tall fences! And I would teach
them just like he had…

*And then, just like that, Fear jumped in as I was
mid-thought!*

"Sir," I mumbled with fright, "I *do* want to do
everything you've said, honestly I do! But I confess

that I'm afraid. What if my neighbors refuse me like I first refused you? I mean, I certainly didn't receive you warmly, or even *well*, for that matter! How is it that you chose to stay and still help me?"

"That's easy, gardener. Just as I know that Pain seeks Pleasure, often in the wrong ways, I also know that Sorrow resists the company of Joy. Although Joy is always the antidote to Sorrow's distress, Sorrow out of its very nature, will frequently oppose the very thing that would set it free. Therefore, gardener, never ask Sorrow if you can come and lend it a helping hand."

"Then what *do* I do?" I asked, feeling uncertain.

"You *resolve* in your heart that you *will* help, in whatever ways are available for you to do so."

"Like you did with me?" I asked.

"Like I did with you." he smiled.

"So…it was my *Sorrow* that resisted your offer of Joy…." I mused, still astonished at such an idea.

"Uh huh. And truthfully, Joy always responds to the cries of Sorrow. But sadly, the eyes and ears of the world's gardeners have been dulled by too much noise, too much busyness. These are the thieves that Accuser uses to keep many from truly seeing and truly hearing. You however, are not to be like this any longer."

"Sir, just who *is* this Accuser that you have spoken of so often?" I asked.

"He's the enemy of your garden….not your trees, not your flowers. Accuser is your only real enemy. He's the one who places upon you the illegitimate demand of *Perfection*, when what you should really strive for is *Excellence*. There is a world of difference between the two; one will bring death and the other will bring life. Therefore, whenever you are tempted to sow and grow only *Perfection*, watch out - that is nothing less than the fiendish whisper of Accuser."

He continued, "Another word of warning gardener, whenever you are tempted to point the finger-of-blame towards another or refuse to take responsibility for your own actions, you are aligning yourself as an ally of Accuser. *Never* listen to his counsel…never follow his guidance, it's always to your disadvantage – and the disadvantage of others – for you to do so!"

Looking around once more, his hands on his hips, he announced, "Gardener, my work here truly is complete."

"But, sir!" I blurted out. "Must you leave so soon?"

He responded to my desperate cry by drawing me into a warm and gentle embrace; one that assured me that we were friends. With a tender smile he placed within my hand the packet of matches that he had just used to create our marvelous bonfire. With a last nod of his head, he turned and began his exit through the huge-and-newly-opened-up-space that had once held my *continuous-nonstop-unbroken-permanent-fence.*

"Sir!" I called out again, tears burning my eyes. "I...I didn't even get your name!"

Turning with a smile, he asked me, "Isn't that obvious, gardener? Do you still not understand?" And with a gleam in his eye and a deepening of his smile, he simply replied, "I am the Master Gardener."

The Master Gardener! Of course! Who else could he be? I was only a gardener, but he was the gardener of all gardeners...he was the Master Gardener!

I cried out in desperation, "But sir, how shall I find you should I have need of you again?! Are you to be found in the local yellow pages?"

He gently laughed as he shook his head. "I will forever be found in the time of your need, even in the gentlest of pleas. I will always let you find me when you search for me. And besides," he said, gesturing towards the matchbook I held, "All you need is already within your hand."

Looking down at the matchbook he'd handed me, I read its cover:

Father & Son Gardening
"Bringing Transformation
To All The World's Gardens"
1-800-PRAY

And as he turned once more to leave, my eyes were drawn to where my journey with him had all begun - the bed of chrysanthemums. What had once been *a bed of dry, spindly, ghastly sticks of wood worthy only of being dug up and put to the fire*, were now regal beauties standing tall and displaying a most wonderful shade of gold. Beyond a doubt, just as the match-cover declared, he had brought *transformation!* My garden and I were perfect testimonies to that very truth, for we had indeed been transformed...by him!

But how? How had he done the *impossible*?!

And whether he read my mind and answered in reply (but once again, that *is* impossible, isn't it?) or whether the night itself responded to my inquiry, I do not know. But this one thing I *do* know! I heard him respond with a call…I heard his joy-filled voice once more riding upon the wind, crying out for all of the world's gardeners who had ears to hear, "Because I am the Life, gardener…*because I Am The Life!*"

Questions of Reflection

Chapter One
A Visitor Comes Calling

1) To what or whom do you liken the visitor to? The gardener to?

2) Have you ever wanted to hide the truth of yourself from others? If so, why?

3) Have you ever felt that no matter how hard you tried to change something about yourself that it was hopeless?

4) Have you ever experienced the tears that the gardener described? What was the event or circumstance that caused them?

5) Have you had a time in your life when you built a self-imposed prison?

Dear Jesus,

There are times I have made a mess of my life and sometimes I feel as if my situation is hopeless! Please give me the eyes to see that with You there is always hope, even if I have built up walls. Thank you Jesus that You are greater than every wall built by man, myself included. Amen.

Notes of Reflection:

Questions of Reflection

Chapter Two
Flower Beds

1) Have you ever experienced a time when someone began to get close to a past event that you had kept hidden away, that you were ashamed of?

2) If so, how did you handle it?

3) Have you ever experienced the pain of someone suggesting that you keep a particular event or situation in the 'dark' – that you keep it a secret? How did that make you feel?

Dear Jesus,

    There are places in the garden of my heart that I am embarrassed for others to see. Thank You for assuring me that there is nothing about me that You are unwilling to forgive, to fix, to heal. Please give me the courage to always trust You. Amen

Notes of Reflection:

Questions of Reflection

Chapter Three
Weeds and Roses

1) Have you ever experienced a time in your life where you believed that things were so bad that there was nothing left to try? Nothing left to be done?

2) Would you say that your heart is more full of Peace or Bitterness?

3) Today, what are some of the 'weeds' that threaten to choke out the peace of your heart?

4) Do you feel as if your true beauty is hidden? If so, by whom or what?

Dear Jesus,

Your ways are so different from my ways. Help me to trust that although You will often-times call me to do things different from the way the world does, that You will help me each step of the way. Help me to let You do what You do best...Love...Heal...Restore. Amen

Notes of Reflection:

Questions of Reflection

Chapter Four
Rocks and Stones

1) Have you ever experienced a time when you resisted the help of someone who wanted to help you? Why do you think you did so?

2) Do you agree that Stubbornness and Pride are merciless when they get into the human heart? Why or why not?

3) Have you ever been faced with the realization that you had a stubborn heart? A prideful heart? If so, how did you deal with it?

Dear Jesus,

I confess that there are times that the ground of my heart is so hard! Please come, and as only You can, restore the condition of my heart, making it worthy of Your good seed. Amen.

Notes of Reflection:

Questions of Reflection

Chapter Five
Conflict

1) Have you ever experienced a time when you were offended by something someone shared with you about yourself, only to find out later that it was true?

2) Have you ever witnessed what you would call a miracle, something that you thought was impossible? If so, what was it?

3) What do you think is the difference between legitimate shame vs. illigitmate shame?

4) Have you ever experienced a time when you felt immediate peace after surrendering an emotion such as anger or unforgiveness?

Dear Jesus,

> *There are times when such a battle is raging within me! Sometimes it's so hard for me to know if I'm justified in the way I feel or if I'm simply being stubborn or prideful. Please help me to surrender everything to You so that I can walk with You in obedience and peacefulness. Amen*

Notes of Reflection:

Questions of Reflection

Chapter Six
Seeds

1) Do you have a vision for your life? If so, write what it is below. If not, spend some time in prayer asking God what His vision for you is. Read Jeremiah 29:11 and allow yourself to be encouraged by the promises that He has for you.

2) List 3 things that need to be accomplished so that you can achieve your vision and make it a reality.

3) If thoughts are seeds, what is it that you are planting? What harvest can be expected?

Dear Jesus,

I need Your vision for my life. Help me to trust that whatever You desire for my life will always be more satisfying than what I could ever desire for myself, more than I could ever hope to achieve on my own. Lord, You know the hurting places of my heart that hold me back from fully trusting, fully loving or allowing myself to be fully loved. Help me Jesus to endure the work that must be done within so that I might experience true liberation, so that I might fully love like You. And Lord, I ask that I would be found faithful to plant seeds that will reap a harvest of Life! Amen

Notes of Reflection:

Questions of Reflection

Chapter Seven
Boulder-dash

1) Can you describe a time when you dealt with righteous anger?

2) Have you personally ever been driven away from someone because their anger was so toxic?

3) Has *your* anger ever driven someone away?

4) What are you currently angry about or who are you angry with?

5) List 4 things that you can do to move your anger to a 'shady place' in your heart.

Dear Jesus,

Sometimes life is so hard! There are so many times I've felt helpless! I think that this is oftentimes the reason for my anger. I know how much other people's anger injures me; please help me to not do the same in return. Please continue to teach me to forgive and be reconciled so that I don't spend a lifetime of driving others away. Thank you, Lord. Amen

Notes of Reflection:

Questions of Reflection

Chapter Eight
Roots, Tending Them

1) What might be some examples of *living* water?

2) What might be some examples of *polluted* water?

3) If *leaves* equal *words*, what are yours saying?

4) If *limbs* equal *actions*, what are yours saying?

5) If *bark* equals *attitudes*, what are yours saying?

6) What emotion has most watered your thoughts recently?

Dear Jesus,

I first want to say Thank You for doing such a good work in me and in my life, even when I don't know it or acknowledge it. Lord, I want my words, actions and attitudes to reflect a heart that is gentle, kind and full of integrity...as well as loyal, strong and courageous. Please help me to discern the pure from the polluted, and once having discerned, to always draw only from the pure. Amen

Notes of Reflection:

Questions of Reflection

Chapter Nine
Roots, Removing Them

1) Has there ever been a time in your life when you felt unproductive?

2) Have you ever endured a time of pruning in your life? What was that like? What was the eventual outcome?

3) What does the following phrase mean to you: "Every gardener must invest everything into Truth and Love for they are of the greatest value."

4) Do you believe that it is possible that someone has paid for you the debt required to acquire Truth and Love?

Dear Jesus,

I confess that there have been times when I've failed, perhaps even refused, to bear the fruit of Service to You or others. I'm so thankful that You are patient with me and yet I know that you are waiting for me to do what I have been created for: to walk in Truth and Love. Thank You that through your self-less sacrifice of Love, You have made it possible for me to acquire what is absolutely priceless. I receive your gifts Lord with a grateful and joy-filled heart. Amen

Notes of Reflection:

Questions of Reflection

Chapter Ten
And The Walls Came Tumbling Down!

1) Have you ever experienced a time when your 'little hammer' was sufficient for a huge task that you needed to accomplish?

2) What healing have you received that you need to share with others? What are some practical ways that you can share that healing?

3) Do you believe the following statement: "When one gives their heart, they in truth give everything." Why or why not?

4) Does the fear of rejection keep you from approaching people who may need your help? If so, how can you work to overcome this?

5) Why do you think that Sorrow resists Joy?

Dear Jesus,

You truly are the great transformer of lives! I confess the times that You have tried to bring me Joy in times of Sorrow and I have resisted. I now know that your Joy is my only real source of hope and help. As best as I know how, I surrender to You and the beautiful work of transformation that You want to accomplish in me. I don't want to any longer resist you – for You alone are what I need. You are the Master Gardener who walks the garden of my heart and I love you. Amen

Notes of Reflection:

Printed in the United States
200804BV00001B/70-174/A